MASTER
Your Mind

Get You Mind To Work for You!

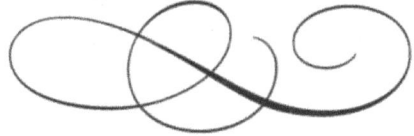

Harrison S. Mungal, Ph.D, Psy.D

Master Your Mind

Copyright © 2024 Harrison S. Mungal

Contact author via email: info@harrisonmungal.com
info@agetoage.ca
www.agetoage.ca
www.harrisonmungal.com
www.harrisonmungalbooks.com
Facebook: Harrison Mungal
Twitter: AgeToAgeInc1
LinkedIn: Harrison Mungal, Ph.D., PsyD
YouTube: Harrison Mungal
Phone: 905-533-1334

ABOUT *the* AUTHOR

Harrison Sharma Mungal, BTh, MCC, MSW, PhD, PsyD

Harrison Sharma Mungal, possessing dual doctoral distinctions in Clinical Psychology and Philosophy in Social Work, demonstrates an unwavering commitment to ameliorating the well-being of his clients. Renowned internationally for his profound insights into cognitive therapy, his expertise spans mental health, addiction, relationships, and family dynamics.

In his role as a highly sought-after workshop presenter, Dr. Mungal extends his practical approach to assisting individuals, couples, families, and corporations. His global influence is evident through engaging presentations at conferences, seminars, and media platforms, where he adeptly integrates humor and enthusiasm into nuanced discussions on mental health, addiction, relationships, and parenting.

Dr. Mungal's innovative and scientifically grounded methodology has garnered acclaim, earning him accolades from diverse institutions. He extends his influence through offering training and consultations to a wide array of community partners, including esteemed professionals in the medical, social work, first responder, law enforcement, and senior management domains.

Actively involved in pioneering cognitive research, Dr. Mungal leads ground-breaking studies addressing mental health challenges such as addiction, psychosis, anxiety, and depression. His work includes the exploration of practical applications, exemplified by initiatives like music therapy for schizophrenia, substance abuse and addictions in the food service industry, and vaccination protocols for young children.

With over two decades of professional acumen, Dr. Mungal has left an indelible mark on the fields of mental health and psychiatry, providing services to diverse communities impacted by brain injuries, refugees, victims of warfare, and individuals in crisis. His pragmatic therapeutic repertoire encompasses evidence-based treatments like Cognitive Behavioural Therapy (CBT), Cognitive Processing Therapy (CPT), Dialectical Behavioural Therapy (DBT), Thought Developmental Practice (TDP) and Acceptance and Commitment Therapy (ACT).

TABLE *of* CONTENT

INTRODUCTION

Welcome to "Master Your Mind" In this booklet, we will make self-discovery and empowerment, as we take a transformative exploration of the mind, delving into its complexities, challenges, and boundless potential. Through a series of insightful chapters, we will uncover the keys to mastering our minds, cultivating clarity, resilience, and a deep sense of inner peace.

The journey to mastering our minds begins with understanding its intricate workings and learning how to harness its power. In this chapter, we'll explore the fundamental principles of mental mastery, including the importance of awareness, self-regulation, and positive thinking. By mastering our minds, we can unlock the door to a life filled with purpose, passion, and unlimited potential.

To master our minds, we must first seek to understand them. In this chapter, we'll delve into the inner workings of the mind, exploring its various layers, functions, and influences. From the subconscious mind to the power of conditioning, we'll unravel the mysteries of consciousness and gain insight into what drives our thoughts, emotions, and behaviors.

One of the greatest challenges on the path to mastering our minds is dealing with mental noise – the endless chatter of thoughts, worries, and distractions that can cloud our judgment and overwhelm our senses. In this chapter, we'll explore strategies for quieting the noise and cultivating inner peace, including mindfulness practices, meditation techniques, and the art of letting go.

In today's fast-paced world, burnout has become an all-too-common phenomenon, affecting individuals of all ages and backgrounds. In this chapter, we'll examine the causes and consequences of burnout and explore strategies for preventing and overcoming it. From setting healthy boundaries to practicing self-care, we'll discover how to protect our minds from the perils of stress and exhaustion.

At the heart of mental mastery lies a deep sense of faith and trust in a higher power. In this final chapter, we'll explore the transformative power of cultivating a God-centered mindset. From surrendering to divine guidance to aligning with divine truths, we'll uncover the keys to unlocking the full potential of our minds and living a life rooted in purpose, passion, and divine grace.

As we embark on this journey to master our minds, let us remember that the power to transform our lives lies within us. By understanding the complexities of the mind, quieting its noise, preventing burnout, and cultivating a God-centered mindset, we can unlock the door to a life of fulfillment, joy, and inner peace. So, let us embrace the journey with open hearts and curious minds, knowing that with dedication and perseverance, we can master our minds and create the life of our dreams.

MASTER *Your* MIND

The mind is the most powerful gift we were created with, along with the heart, and if we don't use our minds correctly, it can be highly destructive. The thoughts that flow through our minds can either be a blessing or a curse. The thoughts we entertain affect our perception and how we interpret information. We all struggle from time to time with our complex thinking patterns, however, with the help of divergent thinking, we can set our minds free.

We need to let our thoughts flow smoothly but should not allow them to rule us. Our thoughts can run wildly if we do not take control of them. Controlling our thoughts is like raising children. If we don't master parenting, our children will walk all over us. They will then bring shame and disrespect upon themselves and their families. Similarly, lacking control over the mind will bring negative consequences. Unwanted thoughts that reside in our mind, will create unproductive and unhealthy thinking. Changing our thinking to dispel such thoughts will eventually allow us to control our behaviours.

Mastering the mind involves managing the thoughts that flow through the mind. It involves reprogramming our thinking. This takes skill and like any talent must be developed. Mastering the mind is like mastering a career or hobby, except the mind is with us twenty-four-seven.

Learning a language takes time, regardless of who we are and what culture or ethic background we are from. The speak a language with the perfect dialect takes a lot of effort and experience speaking. Similarly, we can master our minds with the same principles. The more effort we give, the less stressful we will be in the process. Everything in life takes time to master like a language. The more we practice speaking it the more fluent it becomes.

When we master our thinking we can actually change our feelings which will enable a greater level of peace in our thought life. We can do two main things to take control of our minds; we can either replace our thinking with new thoughts or we can interrupt our thinking. Both require us to become more aware of impulsivity in our thoughts. When we master our minds, we will finally learn to control our thinking.

There are many thoughts that take up a lot of space in our brains. Like "squatters," who do not have permission to live in the location they chose. Some of our thoughts are there in our minds not because we have consciously given permission, but they came along as a result of past hurts. The more they are fed with negativity they more controls they have and eventually they rule the mind just like a squatter who will take over land or a residence they reside in. In order to take charge, make sure you are the one consciously permitting these thoughts to stay in your mind, otherwise, dispel them.

There is usually a loose conglomeration of thoughts running through our minds that come from words that were spoken to us as children. It is often the case that these words take up space in our minds. These are usually thoughts that have us comparing ourselves with others, believing that we are useless, feeling that we will never succeed, or constantly in a state of trying to fulfill other people's expectations of us. The conglomeration of thoughts that come from rejection and betrayal which creates emotional pain should be discarded ceremoniously like putting an object that represents negativity in a box and burying or burning it. These are the thoughts that cripple us and instead of being a master over our minds, we become a slave to them.

We should never allow our thoughts to make us feel like we are in bondage or like we are a slave to fear and worry. Anger, frustration, emotional pain, and regrets grow when we live in bondage. A lack of motivation, low self-esteem, insecurity, anxiety, depression, passivity, and violent behaviours are all signs that we may be in bondage due to our thoughts. Despite how much effect our thoughts can have on us, we are the masters of what we think. We need to stop ourselves from thinking negatively. Start by saying to yourself " I am in control." We can actually write it down or print on it paper "I am in control" and paste it in places where it is visible to remind ourselves we are in charge of ourselves. We should not be blaming others for our behaviours and actions.

Another behaviour we should avoid is beating up on ourselves. It is okay to admit our flaws and faults and move on. Don't allow thoughts of self-disappointment to stay in your brain. No one can change what has happened, however, we can problem-solve. Therefore, looking for solutions instead of allowing negative thoughts to rule our minds should be our focus when things do not go the way we want them to. Sometimes we are our worst bullies. Don't allow your mind to bully you with negative thoughts.

Some unanswered questions that may help you that is usually asked. "What are some tricks and pointers to becoming masters of your minds?" "How do we get rid of the slave mentality?" "How do we take charge of our thinking?"

Most of us need to change our attitude toward ourselves and others at least at some point in our lives. We need to come to a place in life where we can conclude we don't have all the answers to all of life's problems and we cannot "fix" others who may have wronged us. Let that new positive attitude extend even to our enemies. When we start living in this fashion, we will grasp the basics of mastering our mind.

We should be alert to opportunities, realizing that opportunities may never come by again and take advantage of them when they are in your hands. We may fail, but that's a risk we will have to take. Each failure will draw us closer to the prize. Opportunities will expand our experience and develop our skill set.

We need to accept people for who they are instead of trying to change them to be us. We all do our own assessment of people we meet and make a conscious decision to engage with them or maintain a distance. Accepting the fact that we cannot change anyone but we can work with them is another skill we need in order to master the mind. We can give suggestions and recommendations but cannot make someone become the person we want. A great deal of anxiety comes from feeling a lack of control when people do not behave how we want them to. People may even do things that can negatively influence us. Learning to accept others while being yourself and to let them make their own choices will have a positive impact on your relationship with them which in turn will positively impact your outlook.

When we take responsibility, we set a different paste in life. We create a blue print for others to follow. Regardless of what issues may arise as a result of our participation, we need learn to take responsibility. We could be 100% right or 100% wrong, we should take responsibility in finding a solution rather than blaming others. This shows maturity but it is also a trick to allowing ourselves to learn that we are a master of our lives. So many of us live our lives more or less by ourselves and fail to include others. We need to ask ourselves why? Where did it stem from? We can socialize and engage with others and not allow the power of influence to affect us. We can be in control of our mind, what we think of ourselves and others without allowing fear to control us. We were created to be among others to help with healthy stimulants, which assist with preventative factors that will affect our mental health long term.

We need to maintain a mind of a student. Some of us may give the impression that we know it all and that we have an answer for everything in life, yet our own lives are falling apart. It is only to compensate for self-perceived or actual incompetence. We can learn on a daily basis from other people around us. We may learn minor things or get major revelations, but when we are willing to learn, we will always be one step closer to master what we are learning. Assuming the role of a student allows for new thoughts to replace discarded thoughts as we stay in control of what we allow into our minds.

We also need to maintain a mind of a teacher. One thing observed from teaching is that it forces you to learn. When time is spent preparing a lesson, knowledge is gained. And, when we teach, experience and skills are sharpened. Being a teacher sometimes forces us to take control of what we are saying and how we are saying it to ensure that others receive our message effectively. Find out how we can speak into the lives of others even if it's our love ones. The concept of centering our thoughts around communicating a theme will help us in taking control of our thought life.

When the brain is "infected," things can go awry, and the brain no longer serves its purpose efficiently. Symptoms of thought disorders will result as the brain can no longer "carry a conversation" that is sensible. Our brain is a miracle how it function as it holds more information than we could ever imagine. It houses resources we can tap into in the future in an orderly fashion which enables us to perform various impressive tasks. Think of the first time you tried riding a bike. Your brain needed to recall many thoughts in order to keep the bike upright, and it does not matter how many years later you will still know how to ride a bike.

We can become great servants to our minds if we fail to become masters over it. We may find ourselves feeling we cannot control what we think, do or say, but it is possible with proper discipline. Spend time concentrating and thinking through your thoughts before acting, forming opinions, or communicating opinions. We need to learn how to filter our thoughts if we want to master them.

Mastering our minds draws us closer to the destinies assigned to us. We need to come to a place where we can master our minds, otherwise we will never be at peace with ourselves. We need to control what goes into our mind. If it's not good for you, cut it out otherwise it will become like cancer and can destroy you. Our thoughts based on the five sensory systems which are the precursors to our emotions and the actions we take. Mastering our minds will help us to manage the thoughts that plays in our minds, affecting how we feel, what we do, and what comes out of our mouths.

We should never ignore our "gut feeling." Many times before we feed our thought, we have a "gut feeling" that we ignore. If you don't feel good about something, don't pursue it.

Sometimes it could be something simple like going over to visit a friend. You are aware your friend is into things you have been working on in your personal life (drinking alcohol, using street drugs, pornography, video games, and so on). You are aware every time you visit your friend, you end up doing things you should not do. If you have a "gut feeling", ignore it and put a peace to the warning thoughts by exploring all the things that can go wrong. Be alert and aware. Many of us usually gets trapped into deciding against our "gut feeling," and have regrets.

Some of the choices we make triggers our past creating more psychological issues affecting our mental health. When we develop unhealthy coping strategies, they can become our default mode to cope when under stress. The mind will lead you to fall into old habits. However when we master our mind, we can chose alternatives that are new which we can set as new default modes. The healthy neuropathways. An example would be someone who used to use alcohol to cope. The individual may choose to drink club soda with a lime or lemon to avoid drinking alcohol especially at family events. It is a parallelism to the old pathway. Some individuals may choose to set themselves to have one drink which is monitored by their spouse or family member as a healthy way to drink alcohol, which is another parallelism. Street drugs, misuse of prescription medications, gambling, and other addictions are considered unhealthy copying strategies which need new healthy parallelism to cope with life's stressors.

Another interesting thought is learning to say 'No.' The desire to say "no" when we have all intentions to say "yes". If we yield ourselves to what is being asked that is not in our favour, it may lead us to fall into a trap that stimulates negative thoughts. Learning to say "no" is okay and that is one thought we should have flowing in our minds. Some people say yes all the time working all types of extra shifts, helping others move, going to different functions when asked, making donations to everyone who asks, buying items when on sale, buying from door-to-door sellers, going to their friend's sports games, and so on. Learning to say no will help to stay focused on what is most important. Learning to prioritize what is most important will help to become more progressive in life. And this will be another perfect example of mastering the mind, when not driven by impulsivity.

We need to control our assumptions as they can condition the mind to carry the wrong message. Controlling our thoughts from the assumption of what is being texted, emailed, or on the phone. So many time we make a presumption as to what we read, not knowing the full story or the content of what is being written. Some people may have difficulty expressing themselves over the phone, in texting, and emailing. Developing a thought which is usually negative about a phone call, a text, or an email will play in your mind like a movie. The best is face-to-face or making sure you understand the person you are communicating with before you allow your thought to create a conclusion. It's easy to create thoughts, but they can be very challenging to get rid of.

We need to control planting negative thoughts since they are like weeds that can take over our mind from the fruitfulness of being or staying positive. How many of us try to convince others to like what we like, or steer a conversation for others to adapt or engage in? We then become frustrated when the conversation is not going the way we assumed in our minds. We try to make our only conclusion about what the other person's reaction is, what they may say, their mood, how they dress, and their non-verbal language. We try to control others by how we carry on a conversation and not monitoring that we are the dominant ones in the conversation. We speak words to stir the person's emotion or awaken their thoughts, especially if we know some of their weakness or what they have an interest in. We try to live like sales' people, sharing our thoughts to get others to share and then plant our thought seeds into their minds.

Some of us hide our insecurity by speaking negatively about everyone. We have nothing good to say and allow our thoughts that are being created to be negative. Everyone we speak with, we speak to them about someone else. We only see negative attributes and nothing positive comes out of our month. We may not see it and the people we associate with it would not say anything since they want to hear the gossip. Although they are aware that the person who is speaking negatively is also speaking negatively about them behind their back, they continue to feed the person's ego. Negativity feeds on your life and will draw joy from your heart. It's better to walk away and refocus your thoughts on something healthy for the mind.

We have the ability to be resilient. Which means we can train our minds to stay positive, even as we develop our dreams, set goals for our lives, work on plans, and stay on track. We are in control of our thoughts and can do whatever we put our mind to do. We have more control over our thoughts than we may give ourselves credit for. We need to utilize the power of our thought to change the world around us.

With that being said, we need to manage our impulsivity in making decisions, responding to conversations, buying things and voicing our opinions especially when we were not asked to share it. Some of us can be impulsive and have an automatic reaction when others speak to us. It's like if someone were to attempt to hit us, we block ourselves from being hurt. We have a automatic reaction in which at times we can say things that can be offensive toward others and bring emotional harm to ourselves. We need to learn how to manage these automatic thoughts and allow our emotional skills to be a thicker than tomato skin. We all need to consider how we should respond to others if they enforce their thoughts on us. What would be your reaction and how would you psychologically deal with it? Some of us can be defensive with what we say, harsh, cold, emotionless, and unrealistic. We need to consider what we give out, others will react the same and lash back. We all need to learn to be realistic in how we behave with what we say. We should ask ourselves " is it logical," "are we watching the tone of our voices," "are we being "black and white" in our conversation, not willing to listen to those who are in the grey?" "Are we being mindful that others may have value in what they are saying as much as what we say?"

We need to learn how to be our defense lawyer and cross-exam ourselves to ensure that we are accommodating others as much as we want others to accommodate us. Learning the process of how we think and what we may need to change to associate with others is important, otherwise, we may live with a delusion that others want to be in our presence when in reality they are afraid of telling us the truth of how they feel about us. We need to learn to recognize our limitations and speak to others with an understanding that we can make mistakes and is opened for corrections. We need to acknowledge that others have tons of value to add to the conversation. We will carry a long conversation without making others feel they are walking on eggshells. This is a good sign that we are mastering our minds and taking control of our thoughts.

We need to learn that some things we think, we need to put on the shelf, especially if becomes an obstacle in our relationships with others. Learning that our mind can think faster than we can comprehend and the need not to act on what we think at times is healthy. Mastering the mind gives us that power to be in control, especially when we can remind ourselves that we don't have to give an answer to every question, we don't have to react to every emotion from others, we don't have to be impulsive, and that time is our best friend. We can always give an answer when the dust settles, and we give ourselves some time to process a conversation that may be tense. Mastering the mind is being able to weed out anything that may come across harmful, demanding, questioning, parenting and objective.

UNDERSTAND your MIND

Before we explore the techniques for mastering the mind, it's essential to understand what the mind is and how it functions. The mind is not a static entity but a dynamic and ever-changing landscape of thoughts, emotions, beliefs, and perceptions. It is the seat of our consciousness, the lens through which we interpret the world, and the driving force behind our actions.

The mind operates on multiple levels, from the subconscious, where automatic thoughts and behaviors reside, to the conscious, where we make deliberate choices and decisions. It is influenced by factors, including past experiences, societal conditioning, and genetic predispositions. However, despite these external influences, we have the power to shape and mold our minds through conscious awareness and intentional effort.

Being in control of your mind does not mean suppressing or controlling your thoughts and emotions. Instead, it entails cultivating a sense of inner mastery where you are the observer of your mind rather than being at its mercy. It involves developing the ability to choose your thoughts consciously, respond rather than react to external stimuli, and align your actions with your values and goals.

We need to observe our thoughts and emotions without judgment, creating a space between stimulus and response where you can consciously choose how to react. We need to cultivate self-awareness – the ability to recognize our thoughts, emotions, and patterns of behaviour. Self-awareness allows us to identify limiting beliefs, negative thought patterns, and self-sabotaging behaviours, empowering us to challenge and transcend them.

Training the mind is akin to training a muscle – it requires consistent practice, patience, and discipline. Just as you would exercise regularly to strengthen your body, you must engage in mental exercises to strengthen your mind.

Understanding the mind is like embarking on a journey into the depths of consciousness, unraveling its mysteries and unlocking its potential. At its core, the mind is a complex web of thoughts, emotions, beliefs, and perceptions that shape our reality. It's like a vast ocean, constantly in motion, with waves of thoughts crashing against the shores of consciousness. Our minds are constantly chattering, generating an endless stream of thoughts that can range from mundane to profound, from fleeting to persistent.

But despite its ever-changing nature, the mind tends to cling to patterns and habits, often leading to repetitive thoughts and behaviours. This is where the concept of mindfulness comes into play. Mindfulness is the practice of being fully present and aware of our thoughts, feelings, sensations, and surroundings without judgment or attachment. It's about observing the mind as it is, without trying to control or suppress it.

Awareness is the cornerstone of understanding the mind. By cultivating awareness, we gain insight into the inner workings of our thoughts and emotions. We begin to recognize the patterns and tendencies that drive our behaviour, allowing us to make more conscious choices in our lives.

Emotions play a significant role in shaping our mental landscape. They colour our perceptions, influence our decisions, and impact our overall well-being. But all too often, we allow our emotions to dictate our actions, reacting impulsively without considering the consequences.

Learning to understand and regulate our emotions is essential for mastering the mind. This involves recognizing the underlying triggers and patterns that give rise to specific emotions and developing healthy coping strategies for managing them. Techniques such as deep breathing, mindfulness, and cognitive reframing can help us respond to emotions in a more balanced and constructive manner.

Our thoughts have a profound influence on our mental and emotional well-being. They can either uplift us or drag us down, depending on their quality and content. Negative thought patterns, such as self-doubt, rumination, and catastrophizing, can fuel feelings of anxiety, depression, and stress.

To understand the mind, it's essential to cultivate a positive and empowering mindset. This involves challenging negative thoughts and replacing them with more constructive and affirming beliefs. Techniques such as positive affirmations, gratitude journaling, and cognitive restructuring can help rewire the brain for greater resilience and optimism.

Beliefs are the lenses through which we perceive the world. They shape our attitudes, values, and behaviors, often operating at a subconscious level. Our beliefs can either empower us to reach our full potential or hold us back from realizing our dreams.

To understand the mind, it's crucial to examine and challenge limiting beliefs that may be hindering our growth and success. This involves questioning the validity of our beliefs and exploring alternative perspectives. Through practices such as journaling, introspection, and seeking feedback from others, we can gradually shift our beliefs in a more positive and empowering direction.

Understanding the mind is a lifelong journey, one that requires patience, curiosity, and self-reflection. By cultivating awareness, regulating emotions, nurturing positive thoughts, and challenging limiting beliefs, we can begin to harness the power of our minds to create a life filled with purpose, passion, and fulfillment.

In the theater of our minds, the past often takes center stage, casting its shadow over the present and shaping the narrative of our lives. From childhood wounds to past traumas, from regrets to mistakes, the mind has a way of holding us captive to the ghosts of our history.

We all carry scars from past hurts – words spoken in anger, actions taken in haste, betrayals that cut deep. These wounds, though invisible to the eye, can weigh heavily on the soul, shaping our beliefs, attitudes, and behaviours. Whether it's the pain of rejection, the sting of betrayal, or the ache of loss, past hurts have a way of lingering in the recesses of our minds, coloring our perceptions and influencing our interactions with others.

Trauma is like a dark cloud that hangs over our lives, casting its shadow long after the storm has passed. Whether it's physical abuse, emotional neglect, or witnessing violence, traumatic experiences can leave lasting imprints on the mind and body. They can disrupt our sense of safety, trust, and self-worth, leading to a host of psychological symptoms such as anxiety, depression, and post-traumatic stress disorder (PTSD).

Abuse, whether it's physical, emotional, or sexual, can leave deep scars on the psyche, robbing us of our sense of self and leaving us feeling powerless and broken. The effects of abuse can ripple through every aspect of our lives, affecting our relationships, our self-esteem, and our ability to trust others. And even after the abuse has ended, its legacy can continue to haunt us, fueling feelings of shame, guilt, and self-blame.

Regrets are like anchors weighing us down, tethering us to the past and preventing us from moving forward. Whether it's missed opportunities, wrong choices, or words left unsaid, regrets have a way of gnawing at our conscience and filling us with a sense of longing and remorse. We replay past events in our minds, wishing we could turn back the clock and rewrite history, but alas, the past is immutable, and regrets offer no solace.

Our upbringing lays the foundation for who we become, shaping our beliefs, values, and behaviors from an early age. But for some, childhood is not a time of innocence and wonder but rather one of pain and turmoil. Whether it's growing up in a dysfunctional family, experiencing neglect or abandonment, or witnessing addiction or violence, a poor upbringing can leave deep wounds that linger into adulthood, affecting our relationships, self-esteem, and overall well-being.

Mistakes are an inevitable part of the human experience, yet they can hold immense power over us, shaping our self-image and undermining our confidence. Whether it's a failed relationship, a career setback, or a moral lapse, mistakes can trigger feelings of shame, guilt, and self-doubt, leading us to question our worth and abilities. We replay our mistakes in our minds, berating ourselves for our perceived failures and fearing judgment and rejection from others.

Breaking free from the chains of the past requires courage, resilience, and self-compassion. It's about acknowledging the pain and wounds of the past while refusing to let them define us. It's about reclaiming our power and agency, recognizing that we have the ability to shape our own destiny.

One powerful tool for breaking free from the past is therapy. Therapy provides a safe and supportive space to explore past hurts, traumas, and patterns of behaviour, offering insights and strategies for healing and growth. Another important aspect of breaking free from the past is forgiveness – both of others and ourselves. Forgiveness is not about condoning or excusing past wrongs but rather about releasing the hold that resentment, anger, and bitterness have over us. It's about recognizing that holding onto grudges only perpetuates our own suffering and choosing to let go of the past in order to embrace the present with an open heart and mind.

Additionally, practices such as mindfulness, self-care, and self-compassion can help us cultivate a sense of inner peace and acceptance, allowing us to let go of the past and live more fully in the present. By learning to be gentle with ourselves, practicing gratitude, and nurturing healthy relationships, we can begin to break free from the chains of the past and embrace a future filled with hope, resilience, and possibility.

The past may shape us, but it does not define us. No matter what wounds we carry or mistakes we've made, we have the power to rewrite our story and create a future filled with healing, growth, and transformation. By acknowledging our pain, seeking support, and practicing self-compassion and forgiveness, we can break free from the chains of the past and step into the light of our own resilience and strength.

Imagine, you have a really important presentation. You wake up on the morning of that important day with a million thoughts swirling around in your head. You begin to panic as you are going to have a big presentation at work later in the day and your mind kept jumping from one thing to another. You began to worry about minor things such as your dress or you recall a conversation you recently had with a friend or your thoughts slip towards grocery items you need to buy. As you try to get ready for work, your noisy mind continued to buzz with activity. You couldn't find your car keys, and that just added to the chaos. You may end up feeling like you are in a constant state of distraction, unable to focus on anything for more than a few seconds.

Despite all this, when you finally go to work and sit down at your desk to prepare for the presentation, your mind is still not in the mood to cooperate. Instead of preparing for the presentation, you scroll through social media, check your emails, and did everything that distracts you from the presentation. As the time for the presentation approaches, your anxiety levels skyrocketed. You felt overwhelmed and out of control, unable to quiet your mind and focus on the task at hand. In the end, you feel like you have stumbled through the presentation and have failed to show your best potential. And you know what, this is all because of noisy thoughts that are totally irrelevant to your main goal e.g., excellent presentation. Eventually, these rowdy voices inside your mind initiate a cascade of racing thoughts that not only distract you but will also reduce your productivity. But there is a bright side too and keep in mind, dealing with the noisy mind is not an overnight fix, but over time with some effort, we can quiet our minds and get things done without feeling so scattered and stressed out.

Lack of understanding you mind is like having a messy room with stuff all over the place. It's hard to find what you need, and you end up tripping over things and getting distracted by the clutter. A noisy mind is full of distractions and random thoughts that make it tough to focus and get things done. For example, let's say you're trying to write a paper for school, but your mind keeps wandering off to other topics. Maybe you start thinking about what you're going to have for dinner or replaying a conversation you had with a friend earlier in the day. These thoughts distract you from the task at hand and make it hard to focus on what you need to do. Or, maybe you're in a meeting at work, but your mind keeps jumping to other things. You start thinking about your to-do list or worrying about a deadline that's coming up. Imagine you're trying to study for an exam or you're trying to have a conversation with someone, but your mind keeps jumping to other topics, making it hard to stay on track. Again, these thoughts can pull you away from meetings or exams, or normal conversation with friends, and make it hard to stay present and engaged.

A noisy mind is like when your mind feels like a chaotic mess, full of distractions and random thoughts that make it tough to concentrate on anything. It's like having a radio that won't stop playing, even when you want it to be quiet. It's like having a mental traffic jam, with thoughts and ideas all jumbled up and vying for your attention. It can be frustrating, and exhausting, and make it hard to get things done. And when it's really bad, it can lead to feelings of overwhelm, anxiety, and stress. Overall, a noisy mind is a common experience for many people, but there are strategies and techniques we can use to help quiet your mind and find more focus and clarity.

A noisy mind is a term used to describe a mind that is easily distracted or disrupted by internal and external stimuli, making it difficult to focus or concentrate on a task. It can feel like there's a lot of mental chatter, background noise, or random thoughts running through the mind, making it challenging to think clearly and stay on task. It may be also about feeling anxious or stressed, experiencing racing thoughts or intrusive thoughts, or having difficulty falling asleep due to a busy mind. All of these experiences can make it challenging to think clearly, feel calm and centered, and be productive in daily life.

A noisy mind is like a non-stop party up in there. Thoughts bouncing around like ping-pong balls, ideas swirling like a hurricane, and worries nagging like a pesky mosquito. Sometimes, we feel like we are stuck in an endless loop of overthinking. We try to analyze this situation from every angle, trying to anticipate every possible outcome. And even when we gave up on all possibilities and get exhausted, our brains still won't shut up. But the worst is when our brain decides to remind us of the kind of moments where we cringe just thinking about them. The noise will not stop here; it provokes our brain to suddenly remember every single thing we need to do tomorrow or start worrying about something that happened three years ago. And we just feel like screaming in our brains and making insane requests like "Brain! Can't you just give me a break for five minutes?". Despite all the noise, we know our brain is just trying to keep us safe and make sense of the world around us. But sometimes, we wish it would just take a vacation and give us some peace and quiet.

On top of that, a noisy mind feels like our thoughts are zooming around like a race car and we can't seem to hit the brakes. It's tough to concentrate when our brain keeps throwing new ideas and distractions at us. We even struggle to get some shut-eye because our brains won't quit chattering. There will be unannounced bouts of anxiety, worries, and panic attacks because our brain keeps fixating on potential problems and worst-case scenarios. We're restless and antsy because our brain is always telling us to do something else. Ironically, a noisy mind can also make us feel super tired and drained.

So, you have now got a clear idea of what a noisy mind actually is and if you are also a victim of it. Don't worry, you're not alone. Sometimes our brain can feel like it is on overdrive, churning out thoughts and worries, and ideas faster than we can even process them. It can be frustrating! But, if today, it is dark, then tomorrow, it will be bright, surely. There are certain things we can do to help calm our minds down a bit. Take an example of mindfulness techniques that just means paying attention to the present moment without judgment. We just need to spare a few minutes in 24 hours to try things like deep breathing or meditation and focus on our surroundings and let our thoughts come and go. Or we can opt for journaling. Writing down our thoughts and feelings can be a great way to get them out of our heads and onto paper where we can look at them more objectively. And sometimes, just getting things off our chest can be therapeutic.

Dealing with a noisy mind can be a real challenge, but it's not an insurmountable one. And whatever you do, just remember, don't be too hard on yourself! Everyone has a noisy mind from time to time, and it's okay to take some time to relax and recharge. Whether that means taking a bubble bath, going for a walk, or curling up with a good book, make sure you're taking care of yourself and giving your brain a break when it needs it. With a little bit of effort and patience, you can learn to quiet your mind and find some peace amid the chaos. Whether it's through meditation, deep breathing, or other relaxation techniques, there are plenty of strategies we can try to help calm our thoughts and ease our anxiety. So, lets us make a promise together, don't give up hope - with time and practice, we can learn to silence the noise and find some much-needed tranquility.

A noisy mind, in some instances, indicates something more serious, deeper. We may be blaming it on our tough daily routines but deep inside, it would be a manifestation of something much more serious than that. And on the other hand, what if something more alarming is causing these disturbingly loud noises inside our minds rather than the stress we endure every day due to our busy lives? You might be wondering what would be worse than a 'Noisy mind'? There is something more dangerous than an uncontrolled loud voice inside the mind and that is an 'Emotional wound". Emotional wounds are those painful experiences from our past that have not been fully resolved. They can be caused by a variety of things, such as abuse, neglect, loss, or trauma. These wounds can leave us feeling hurt, angry, or scared, and they can have a lasting impact on our mental health.

One of the ways emotional wounds affect us is by creating a state of hyperarousal in our brains. When we experience a traumatic event or something that is emotionally overwhelming, our brains go into overdrive. We enter a state of fight or flight, where our bodies are flooded with stress hormones like cortisol and adrenaline. This response is designed to help us survive in dangerous situations, but it can also have negative effects on our mental health.

Over time, this hyperarousal can lead to what we call a "noisy mind." Our thoughts become fragmented and disorganized, making it difficult to focus or concentrate. We may experience racing thoughts or a constant stream of mental chatter. We may feel anxious, overwhelmed, or stressed out, even when there is no immediate danger present. So, how do emotional wounds lead to a noisy mind? It all comes down to the way our brains process and store memories. When we experience something traumatic or emotionally overwhelming, our brains store that memory differently than normal memory. It becomes "stuck" in our brains, and we may continue to relive that experience repeatedly.

Lack of understanding you mind can lead to worry and fear. Lack of understanding your mind can lead to worry and fear. But the good news is that there are ways to quiet a noisy mind and heal from emotional wounds. Therapy can be an effective way to process and resolve hurt minds. In severe cases, we can work with a trained therapist and learn how to reframe our experiences and develop new coping strategies. It's important to remember that healing from emotional wounds or a hurt mind takes time and patience. But with the right tools and support, it's possible to quiet a noisy mind and find peace and healing.

BURNOUT MIND

Our mind is the most beautiful, powerful, and extraordinary gift of God. This intellectual body organ is blessed with miraculous autonomy that controls each and every cell of our body and dictates the role of all body parts. Thus, it would not be wrong to say that it is our mind that shapes our destiny and molds our future. Owing to such indispensable importance of the mind, it is our duty to take care of it even more than our body because if the mind is unwell then the body cannot function optimally. We need to take care of the mind.

Although the mind is an exceptionally strong and powerful body organ, it is extremely vulnerable to internal and external stressors. At one moment, our mind is working as the most influential body part and then on the very next moment, it becomes a fragile organ that lost its dominance and eventually "burns out". Now, let's talk about this extreme mental exhaustion known as "Mind Burnout" in detail that will tell us how to spot the signs of mind burnout early and some ways to deal with it.

No doubt, the mind is a total powerhouse, but it can definitely get worn down if we push it too hard for too long. It is like when you have been running on fumes for so long that you just hit a wall, you know how it feels? It is when all that stress and overwork just takes a toll and leaves you feeling drained and disconnected. So, how can you tell if you're experiencing mind burnout? Some common signs include feeling tired all the time, a decrease in performance and productivity, a lack of motivation, and just feeling overall apathetic about things you used to enjoy. If you're feeling these things, it might be time to take a step back and assess your stress levels.

The good news is mind burnout is definitely treatable. There are plenty of ways to manage stress and get back on track. It could be taking a break, trying some self-care activities like exercise or meditation, or even seeing a therapist for some extra support. The most important thing is to listen to your mind and body and take the steps necessary to give yourself the care and attention you need. Don't be afraid to reach out for help when you need it. You got this!

Mind burnout, formally known as *Burnout Syndrome*, is when you're just completely burnt out. We feel exhausted, and mentally drained, and can't seem to get anything done. It's not just about being mentally tired either - our body gets exhausted too. It's important to note that burnout isn't a mental illness. It's just a term to describe a bunch of symptoms that we experience during burnout, and it doesn't happen from just one event. It takes a long time for our minds to get tired from all the worries or stress that attack us from different parts of our life. This can be from things like a tough job, a bad relationship, academic stress, unemployment, and so on. All these things just pile up and wear down our minds, eventually leading to burnout. So, you might be wondering what causes this extremely hazardous exhaustion to mind leading to burnout.

As already mentioned, our mind is very powerful so it will never give up due to everyday stress or busy homework schedules. But when we drown ourselves in worries and forget the importance of mental breaks then our mind eventually gives up. Our mind has to pay the price even if our body is overworking and is not getting much-needed rest. Not only stress and overworking destroy the peace of our mind but our home and working environment also define our mental well-being. We might never be able to flourish our minds if we are living at home where we feel unappreciated and lack love and emotional support or working in an office where we are surrounded by rude and unsupportive colleagues.

It is our mind that can make our lives a living hell or a beautiful paradise. In other words, if we overthink every life situation then we are depriving our strong mind of its energy. We should never ignore one thing, not everything in our life is under control. So, this is utterly useless to overthink things we can't control. Instead, rely on God's decision and believe in your willpower. If we let negative thoughts and feelings take over, our life can start to feel like a living nightmare. But if we focus on positivity and keep a clear head, our life can be a real paradise. It all comes down to what we do with our minds. So, it's important to keep a check on our thoughts and make sure we're not letting the bad stuff take over. We have the ability to rewire the brain to avoid mind burnouts.

In addition to overthinking, the expectations we have from our loved ones and even from ourselves can ruin many beautiful things. Unrealistic expectations from ourselves or trying to fulfill other people's expectations could be mentally draining. So, if we got feeling like our mind is going to black out then we must stop for a few moments and let our mind relax and take rest. Nevertheless, we should prioritize our mental health before anything and then everything else will automatically fall into order.

Mind burnout is no joke; it can really mess with the structure and physiology of our brains. When we're under constant stress, our body pumps out cortisol, the stress hormone, to help us deal with it. But when cortisol levels stay high for too long, it can shrink the size of the hippocampus, the part of the brain that helps with memory and learning, and even stop the creation of new brain cells. Plus, it can damage the prefrontal cortex, the part that helps with decision-making and executive functions. And let's not forget the toll it takes on our sleep. Chronic stress can cause sleep disturbances, like insomnia, which can make our brain feel like mush. Sleep is crucial for the brain to function properly and get rid of waste, so when we don't get enough of it, it can affect our cognitive abilities like attention, memory, and problem-solving.

Besides, burnout also increases the risk of depression and anxiety, which can severely damage our brains permanently. Depression can change brain structure and function, mess with hormone and neurotransmitter levels, and even increase the risk of cognitive decline and memory problems. And anxiety can ramp up activity in the amygdala, the part that processes fear and anxiety, making it harder for our brain to function.

Plus, mental exhaustion can lead to a whole bunch of cognitive problems, like brain fog, making it hard to concentrate and remember things. It can also make it tough to make decisions, plan, and prioritize tasks. And on top of all that, it can suck the motivation and energy right out of us, making us not want to do the things we used to love. This can even reduce brain functioning and damage brain plasticity i.e., the brain's ability to change and adapt.

Mental burnout can show up in some seriously unpleasant ways. Physically, we might be feeling too lazy to do anything, even getting out of bed could be a frightening task. We may notice changes in our eating and sleeping habits and on that, we might suffer from all sorts of aches and pains. On the other hand, our emotions may be riding on a roller coaster. We may encounter dreadful feelings like every day is a bad day, we doubt our abilities and strengths, we get bursts of anger and feel worthless. These emotions make us feel emotionally detached and numb and result in negative self-talk. And, as if that weren't enough, we might also find ourselves struggling with addiction, snapping at others, and feeling distant from those around us. All of this can lead to a drop in productivity, neglecting our responsibilities, and even engaging in dangerous behaviours.

Burnout is when we feel totally drained, mentally and physically exhausted, and just can't seem to get anything done. It could be a real pain in the neck which is an alarming sign for your overall health. It is caused by long-term stress and can come from a bunch of different things like too much thinking, too much stress, peer pressure, trying to do too much at once, a lack of support, unrealistic expectations, and health problems. The important thing is to watch out for the signs of burnout and get help if needed and don't worry, we can prevent it from happening. Yes, we can protect ourselves by taking care of our body and mind with the help of simple things like exercise, eating right, relaxing, and being mindful. And if mental fatigue is getting out of hand, it is absolutely fine to see a therapist or get help from the doctor. Nevertheless, mind burnout is a warning sign that indicates something needs to change, and if we ignore it, things could get really bad and really fast. Thus, taking a few simple steps can go a long way in keeping our minds and body healthy.

Have you ever felt completely and utterly exhausted, like you've been running on empty for far too long? That's burnout. It's when you've been pushing yourself so hard for so long that you're just done; Burned out! It can happen in any area of life – work, school, relationships, you name it. While, on the other hand, when you have experienced some kind of trauma or injury that's left a lasting impact on your mental health. This could be things like abuse, neglect, exposure to violence, traumatic events, and more. Such events could leave your mind with wounds that may provoke other serious mental symptoms like anxiety, depression, fear, guilt, and shame.

If we look deep into the valleys of a burnout mind and a wounded mind, we can see that both these mind conditions share the same roots. Well, burnout is more about being exhausted from overdoing it, while a wounded mind is about experiencing something traumatic that's left a lasting impact. But, it's important to note that the two have the same origin and can even overlap – someone with a wounded mind may also experience burnout, and someone with burnout may develop symptoms of a wounded mind. But the good news is, both burnout and a wounded mind are treatable. Whether it's taking time to rest and recharge, seeking support from a therapist, or trying self-care techniques, there are ways to help. The key is to listen to your body and mind and seek help when you need it.

Although a burnout mind and a wounded mind may have the same manifestations, they are actually two different things. By understanding the difference and knowing what steps to take, you can start on the path to a happier, healthier mind.

Do you ever feel like your mind is just too cluttered with information that you feel like being mentally stuck in traffic during rush hour? This feeling is common when we try to do too much at once or take in too much information. Under such situations, our brains can start to feel overwhelmed and congested, making it harder to focus, remember things, and make decisions, in short, there's just too much going on at once, and it can be hard to make progress. Like there's too much going on up there and you just can't seem to focus. You know the one - where your brain just feels overwhelmed, and like you're never going to get anything done. This is like your brain is "congested" due to a lot of unresolved thoughts that pile up and disturb your inner peace. It is a common experience for many of us in our fast-paced and information-packed world, but luckily, there are ways through which we can clear the clutter and give our brain the boost it needs to power through.

Our brains are incredibly powerful and capable of handling a lot of information at once, but there's a limit to what we can process effectively. Now, let us dig deep into circumstances that cause our brains to mess up and develop congestion. There are a lot of different factors that can contribute to that cluttered feeling, from stress and anxiety to multitasking and information overload. Brain congestion can be a real pain, and it can make it difficult for us to focus, think clearly, and get things done. There are a number of different things that can cause brain congestion, and 'stress' being the biggest one.

When we're under a lot of stress, our brains can become congested and overwhelmed. This is because stress triggers the release of cortisol, a hormone that can interfere with the normal functioning of our brains. When cortisol levels are high, we may find it difficult to focus, concentrate, or remember things. This is why it's important to manage stress as much as possible, whether through exercise, meditation, or other stress-relieving activities. Stress not only 'congests' your mind space but it will also mess up your sleeping schedules.

Lack of sleep is another reason why your brain gets stuffed with racing thoughts. When we don't get enough sleep, our brains don't have the chance to recharge and repair themselves. This can lead to a build-up of toxins in the brain, which can interfere with its normal functioning. In addition, lack of sleep can impair cognitive function and make it harder for us to think clearly and make good decisions. To avoid brain congestion due to lack of sleep, it's important to make sure you're getting enough sleep each night.

This is not only stress and sleep that scramble your brain but a poor diet can also contribute to brain congestion. Like our bodies, our brains also need food to flourish, and that comes from our diet. When we don't eat a healthy, balanced diet, our brains don't get the nutrients they need to function properly. This can lead to brain fog, fatigue, and difficulty concentrating. In addition, consuming too much sugar or caffeine can lead to spikes and crashes in energy levels, which can make it difficult to focus and think clearly. But if we add more greens and fruits to our diet, our mind will ultimately reward us by being in a healthy state and functioning at its best. Just like whatever we eat fuels our brain, what we drink lubricates our mind's machinery.

Not drinking enough water dehydrates our minds and this dehydration can interfere with normal functioning. Brain fog, headaches, lack of focus, difficulty in concentration, and ambiguous thoughts are all the aftermaths of poor diet and not drinking enough water. Similarly, too much alcohol can also exploit our minds and give rise to uncontrolled racing thoughts. We just cannot put all blame on ourselves and fall into the wrong perception that stress, diet, or lifestyle habits, which are somehow under our control, are narrowing our minds. But the biggest role in brain congestion is often played by the environment we live in and the people we interact with every day. You know, being in a supportive environment, surrounded by loving family, and having friends that will always have your back is the biggest determinant of your professional success and personal development. When we know we have someone to talk to without any hesitation, we will never have to put a barrier to our unbridled thoughts and thus, they can flow smoothly. On the other hand, when we are living in a house where others are emotionally unavailable or our emotional needs are often ignored, then our brain will lose its authority and the result will be a build-up of unsettled thoughts in an already crowded mind.

Likewise, when our friendships and social connections are artificial or fake then it would be an absolute threat to our mental and even physical growth. So, use your all senses and choose wisely. Remember, not every person with whom you shake hands is your friend. Some might be your enemy in a disguise and they will always try to drag you down. They will hurdle your way to success and strain your mental and emotional health. One more thing, here the environment is not limited to friends and family. Instead, there are several physical factors that could be extremely traumatizing to our brains and congest our thinking. For example, when we get exposed to toxins, such as lead, mercury, or pesticides, our brain function suffers a decline and leads to brain congestion. In addition to this, exposure to loud noises or bright lights can be overwhelming for the brain and lead to fatigue and difficulty concentrating. To avoid brain congestion due to environmental factors, it's important to minimize your exposure to toxins and take breaks from loud or bright environments when possible.

One of the biggest reason why you just cannot think straight is making your brain brimful of unnecessary thoughts. You might be wondering what else is left now but the biggest contributor to brain congestion is still yet to unveil and that is 'medical conditions.' There is a huge list of illnesses that could lead to chemical imbalances in our brains, for example, conditions like ADHD, anxiety, and depression can interfere with brain function and make it difficult to focus and concentrate. In addition, certain medical conditions, such as migraines or concussions, can cause headaches and other symptoms that can interfere with brain function. These are alarming conditions that are bound to have hazardous side effects on physical as well as mental health. But we will not go deep into these medical situations as these health concerns are not manageable by merely reading a book. And if you suspect that the weird feelings of brain congestion are due to some sort of underlying medical pathology, then rush to your doctor at once.

So, along with stress, poor sleep, bad food, no water, and bad surroundings, there are some medical conditions that can clog up our brains. But if we know what causes these clogs and we take immediate action, we can keep our brains in tip-top shape. Always keep this thing in your mind; you should be your top priority, so, take care of yourself and if you're feeling brain fog for a long time or other issues that get in the way of your day, get help!

No doubt, a congested brain would lead us nowhere. Instead, it would put a barrier to our professional and personal success. But there is no need to worry at all! If you feel like you are drowning in the deep oceans where waves of unsettled thoughts are continuously hitting your ship then, stop here. Take a deep breath and instead of running out of the ocean, crawl through it. If we try to rush through life's obstacles, we would be indirectly fanning the flames that may explode if we keep adapting to such wrong approaches. So, what you should be doing if you're feeling like your brain is all congested and don't know how to crawl through it? As we already learn, brain congestion is like our thoughts are stuck in traffic and can't seem to get moving, so what we can do to get out of a traffic jam and reach our destination on time? Well, don't worry, there are plenty of things we can do to clear up the mess and empty our brains and think clearly.

Listen, we are just too busy and we have a lot on our plate but sometimes we just need to step away from it all for a bit. Take a breath and do something else for a few minutes. It doesn't have to be anything fancy, just something to clear our heads. Go for a walk, take some deep breaths, meditate, or just sit and stare out the window. In the end, you would be surprised at how much better you will feel after a short break. And yes, also learn to prioritize things. We all have a million things we need to do, but trying to do them all at once is a recipe for disaster. Instead, focus on the most important tasks first and give them your full attention. Once you've completed those, move on to the next most important tasks. This will help you stay organized and on track, which will make everything feel less overwhelming.

Sometimes, we intentionally make our life complicated and tough, and things can get too overwhelming, ultimately leading to brain fog. Therefore, adapt simplicity. Try to simplify your tasks or information by breaking things down into smaller, more manageable pieces. Try to eliminate anything that's not essential and focus on the things that really matter. This will help clear the clutter and make it easier to think. Simplifying things will open doors to an organized lifestyle. A messy and cluttered physical space can contribute to a messy and cluttered mental space. Take some time to organize your workspace, declutter your surroundings, and make sure everything has a designated place. Having a clear and organized physical environment can reduce stress and make it easier to focus.

Now, here comes an important step towards an optimal body and a clear mind. You might get offended by this because when the mind is already tired, the body will also give up. But exercise is the biggest antidote for a crowded mind. Your first expression after reading this might be, "Ugh, exercise? That's the last thing I want to do when my brain is already tired!" But trust me, exercise can do wonders for your mental clarity. It releases endorphins, which can help boost your mood and make you feel more alert. Plus, it gets your blood flowing, which can help bring more oxygen to your brain and help you think more clearly. Exercise also helps us in getting a good night's sleep. Sleeping well is another way to clear up your mind because it is no secret that lack of sleep can mess with your brain. Make sure you're getting enough rest each night (aim for at least 7-8 hours) and try to stick to a consistent sleep schedule. If you're having trouble sleeping, try some relaxation techniques like deep breathing or meditation before bed.

And now, let's talk about neglected things that are messing with your mind and making it overcrowded with unwanted thoughts. These overlooked factors encompass your eating habits and the amount of water your drink every day. Eat a healthy diet because our brain needs fuel to function properly, so we should make sure we are giving it the right kind of fuel. Eat a balanced diet that includes plenty of fruits, vegetables, whole grains, lean proteins, and healthy fats. Avoid processed foods, sugar, and excessive amounts of caffeine, which can all contribute to brain fog. Comparably, dehydration can also contribute to brain fog, so make sure you're drinking plenty of water throughout the day. Aim for at least eight glasses of water a day, and don't forget to drink more if you're exercising or in a hot environment.

Nevertheless, take time for yourself each day to do something you enjoy, whether it's reading a book, taking a bubble bath, or going for a walk. And don't forget to laugh.

Laughter is a great stress reliever and yes, the best medicine! These are just a few of the strategies we can use to clear brain congestion and boost our brainpower. The key is to find what works for us and make it a regular part of our routine. With a little effort and a lot of self-care, we can keep our brains running smoothly and avoid getting stuck in mental traffic.

Just keep in mind, brain congestion is not dangerous if we detect it early and take reasonable steps to cope with it. As you have already read, brain congestion is like a traffic jam. If we get out of our homes on time then we can avoid traffic jams and reach our destination on time. Similar is the case with the crowded brain. If we take appropriate and timely action against messy or unnecessary thoughts, we can make our minds a paradise to live with. But in today's fast-paced and highly competitive world, we get strangled into the rat race and are too busy to take of ourselves. We get too occupied with worldly stuff that we completely ignore ourselves. Whether it is our physical health, spiritual self, or our mental wellness, each and every element of our existence is paying the price. And undoubtedly, our mind has to pay the biggest price.

We cannot see our emotions and detect ups and downs in our mental state like we can monitor our blood glucose levels or assess changes in blood pressure. Therefore, our thoughts are more susceptible to everyday stress and become dangerously uncontrollable leading to overthinking, depression, and anxiety disorder. This uncontrollable stuffing of our minds with racing thoughts not only 'congests' our thinking capacity but can also lead to 'combustion'. The literal meaning of combustion is

"Burning" and the same goes for our minds. When our minds become overloaded with thoughts, 'brain congestion' will take place which will ultimately result in a 'meltdown'. Brain combustion is another indicator that something is messing with your brain, and it needs immediate attention, otherwise, the aftermaths would be worse than you can imagine.

GOD-CENTERED MINDSET

In the vast landscape of the mind, our thoughts wield tremendous power. They shape our perceptions, influence our emotions, and ultimately determine the quality of our lives. When our thoughts are positive and empowering, they serve as a catalyst for growth, resilience, and success. However, when our minds are clouded by negativity and self-doubt, they can become a prison, holding us back from reaching our full potential

Our thoughts are like seeds planted in the fertile soil of our minds. They have the power to blossom into reality, shaping the course of our lives in profound ways. When we dwell on negative thoughts, such as self-criticism, doubt, and fear, we create a breeding ground for suffering and limitation. These thoughts become like chains, binding us to the past and inhibiting our ability to move forward with confidence and purpose.

But just as negative thoughts can hold us captive, positive thoughts have the power to set us free. By cultivating a mindset rooted in positivity and faith, we can break free from the bonds of self-doubt and embrace a life of abundance and fulfillment.

Positive affirmations are simple yet powerful statements that are repeated regularly to affirm positive beliefs about oneself or one's circumstances. They serve as a tool for reprogramming the subconscious mind, replacing negative self-talk with empowering beliefs and attitudes.

For example, instead of saying, "I'm not good enough," you might affirm, "I am worthy and deserving of love and success." By repeating this affirmation consistently, you begin to shift your mindset from one of self-doubt to one of self-worth and confidence.

At the heart of a positive mindset lies a deep sense of faith and trust in a higher power. Whether you refer to this power as God, the Universe, or the Divine, cultivating a God-centered mindset involves surrendering to a greater wisdom and purpose beyond our own understanding.

A God-centered mindset is one that recognizes that we are not alone in our journey, that there is a guiding force greater than ourselves that is always working for our highest good. It's about letting go of the need to control every outcome and instead placing our trust in the divine plan unfolding in our lives.

One way to cultivate a God-centered mindset is by aligning our thoughts and beliefs with divine truths. These truths are timeless principles that reflect the nature of God and the universe, such as love, abundance, and forgiveness.

For example, instead of dwelling on past mistakes and regrets, we can affirm the divine truth of forgiveness, recognizing that we are worthy of redemption and second chances. Instead of worrying about the future, we can affirm the divine truth of abundance, trusting that God will provide for our needs.

Another key aspect of a God-centered mindset is surrendering to divine guidance. This involves relinquishing our ego-driven desires and allowing ourselves to be led by the wisdom of the divine. It's about letting go of the need to have all the answers and instead trusting that God's plan for us is far greater than anything we could imagine.

Cultivating a God-centered mindset means living in alignment with divine will. This involves surrendering our own agendas and desires and allowing ourselves to be vessels for God's love and light in the world. It's about using our gifts and talents to serve others and make a positive impact, knowing that we are co-creators with the divine in manifesting goodness and abundance.

Cultivating a God-centered mindset is a journey of faith and surrender, one that requires courage, humility, and trust. By aligning our thoughts and beliefs with divine truths, surrendering to divine guidance, and living in alignment with

God's will, we can break free from the chains of self-doubt and embrace a life of purpose, passion, and fulfillment.

Through the practice of positive affirmations and the cultivation of a God-centered mindset, you can unlock the limitless potential that resides within your soul and create a life filled with joy, abundance, and God's grace.

Our brains are incredibly adaptable organs, capable of forming new connections and rewiring themselves in response to our experiences and environment. This phenomenon, known as neuroplasticity, holds the key to unlocking our potential for growth, healing, and transformation.

Conditioning refers to the process of training or programming the mind to respond in a certain way to stimuli or experiences. From an early age, we are conditioned by our upbringing, environment, and life experiences to develop certain patterns of thinking, feeling, and behaving. These conditioning factors can shape our beliefs, attitudes, and perceptions, often without us even realizing it.

Unfortunately, many of us are conditioned to focus on the negative aspects of life, dwelling on past hurts, traumas, and failures. This negative conditioning can create a cycle of self-limiting beliefs and behaviors that hold us back from reaching our full potential.

The good news is that just as we can be conditioned for negativity, we can also be conditioned for positivity. By intentionally focusing on positive thoughts, emotions, and experiences, we can rewire the brain's neural pathways, creating new patterns of thinking and behaving that support our well-being and success.

One powerful way to condition the mind for positivity is by practicing gratitude. Gratitude is the practice of acknowledging and appreciating the blessings and abundance in our lives, no matter how small or seemingly insignificant they may be. By regularly expressing gratitude, we train our brains to focus on the positive aspects of life, shifting our perspective from one of scarcity to one of abundance.

Optimism is another key component of positive conditioning. Optimists tend to see setbacks and challenges as temporary and manageable, viewing them as opportunities for growth and learning. By cultivating an optimistic mindset, we can reframe negative experiences in a more positive light, allowing us to bounce back from adversity with resilience and grace.

Our environment plays a significant role in shaping our mindset and outlook on life. Surrounding ourselves with positive influences, such as supportive friends, inspiring mentors, and uplifting content, can help reinforce our commitment to positivity and create an atmosphere conducive to growth and transformation.

In addition to cultivating positive thoughts and emotions, it's essential to challenge and reframe negative beliefs that may be holding us back. Negative beliefs, such as "I'm not good enough" or "I'll never succeed," create self-fulfilling prophecies that reinforce our sense of inadequacy and failure. By identifying and challenging these beliefs, we can replace them with more empowering and affirming beliefs that support our goals and aspirations.

Conditioning the mind for positivity is not a one-time event but rather a lifelong journey. It requires consistency, persistence, and dedication to cultivating a mindset of growth and possibility. Just as physical exercise strengthens our bodies over time, mental conditioning strengthens our minds, creating new neural pathways that support our well-being and success.

Conditioning the mind for positivity is a powerful tool for rewiring the brain and breaking free from the shackles of the past. By practicing gratitude, cultivating optimism, surrounding ourselves with positivity, challenging negative beliefs, and maintaining consistency and persistence, we can create a mindset that is resilient, optimistic, and empowered to create the life we desire.

We can gain a deeper inside into thinking patterns and how we can trick our minds into following our orders. No doubt, this all will take considerable practice, hard work, and strong determination but believe me, once you achieve this, you can even 'Renew your mind .'Here renewing our minds means regaining access to the mental potential with which we are born. The strength God has blessed us, but we have lost it in the woods of life, surrounded by anxiety, stress, failure, money problems, and relationship issues. But don't worry; we can get it back. There will be some ups and downs in this journey, but in the end, the victory will be ours! So, let's finish this magical journey by 'renewing our minds.'

Our lives are under the continuous transition between sunny days and gloomy evenings. We often feel bogged down by the stresses and worries of daily life. We can easily get caught up in negative thoughts and emotions that just won't seem to go away. Well, this is the sign- it's time to renew your mind! Renewing your mind is all about taking a step back and clearing out all the mental clutter and negativity that is holding you back. It's about finding ways to refresh your mindset and approach life with a more positive, focused outlook. It takes effort and commitment, but the benefits are well worth it in the end! But trust me, it's easier than you might think, and ultimately, renewing our minds is all about living a more fulfilling and joyful life.

Renewing minds is not a single technique; instead, it is an ongoing process that is based on several strategies that target our mental and physical selves. For example, there are days when we go through a really tough time and are haunted by feelings of being overwhelmed and stressed. We just can't shake the negative thoughts that dominate our heads. In such a situation, we need some ways that not only provide escape but will help in regaining control of our minds. For this, practicing mindfulness and meditation, and deep breathing exercises can make a huge difference. By eradicating unwanted thoughts and focusing on the present moment, we can feel more centred and calmer. And if we combine them with journaling, we can work through our emotions and gain a better sense of clarity about what we need to do to improve our situation.

Our next-door neighbour recently lost her loved one in a tragic car accident that added fuel to the fire. Stress, anxiety, and PTSD were attacking her from all directions, and she was on the verge of giving up. She had tried all sorts of things to manage her symptoms, but nothing seemed to provide significant relief. Then after the recommendation of her therapist, she began to work on renewing her brain along with other ongoing treatments. She started practicing gratitude - every day. She would make a list of things she was thankful for, no matter how small they might seem. Over time, she found that this simple practice helped her feel more positive and empowered, and it helped her shift her mindset away from the negative thoughts that were holding her back. So, the moral of the story is whether we're dealing with stress, anxiety, or just feeling stuck in a rut, renewing our minds can be a powerful way to break free and start living our best life.

There are many different techniques we can use to renew our minds, depending on what works best for us. Some people find it helpful to practice meditation or mindfulness, which can help them calm their thoughts and find a sense of inner peace. Others might find that journaling or "brain dumping" their thoughts onto paper can help them sort through their feelings and come to a better understanding of themselves.

Some people have engaged in activities that help them reframe their mindset and cultivate a more positive outlook. This included practicing gratitude, setting intentions, or doing things that bring them joy and fulfillment. Sometimes it's as simple as taking a break from social media or other sources of negativity and instead focusing on the people and things that make you feel happy and uplifted. Ultimately, renewing your mind takes effort and commitment, but the benefits are well worth it in the end!

Renewing our minds encompasses the processes that change our thought patterns and perspectives and improve our mental and emotional well-being. It involves intentionally replacing negative, self-limiting beliefs and thought patterns with positive, empowering ones. Renewing our minds means shifting our focus from what's wrong in our lives to what's right and from what we can't do to what we can do.

Renewing our minds is good for a multitude of reasons. First and foremost, our mind is the epicentre of our thoughts, emotions, and actions. If we allow our minds to become stagnant, it can lead to negative thinking patterns, low self-esteem, and a lack of motivation. By renewing our minds, we can break out of these negative cycles and improve our mental health. Secondly, renewing our minds can also help us to develop a growth mindset. This means that we see challenges as opportunities for growth and learning rather than obstacles to be avoided. When we renew our minds, we become more open to new ideas, experiences, and perspectives. This can help us to become more creative, innovative, and adaptable.

Another benefit is that it can improve our relationships. When we have a negative mindset, we may be more prone to conflict, misunderstandings, and judgment. However, when we renew our minds, we become more empathetic, compassionate, and understanding. This can help us to build stronger connections with the people in our lives, whether it be our family, friends, or coworkers. Working on our minds opens the door to personal growth and development. When we take the time to reflect on our thoughts and behaviours, we can identify areas where we may need to improve. This can help us to break bad habits, overcome fears, and develop new skills. As a result, we can become more confident, resilient, and successful.

So how do we renew our minds? There are many different strategies that can be effective, depending on your preferences and needs. Some of you may find that meditation, journaling, or therapy can help you clear your mind and gain perspective. While others may benefit from engaging in creative activities, such as writing, painting, or music. Still, others may find that exercise, healthy eating, and adequate sleep can improve their mental clarity and well-being. Whatever path you select, the only key to renewing our minds is to be intentional and consistent. It's not a one-time event but rather a continuous process of self-reflection and growth. By making a habit of renewing our minds, we can improve our mental and emotional health, build stronger relationships, and achieve our goals and aspirations. So why not give it a try?

If you further explore the effects of mind renovation, you would be surprised to know that renewing our minds can actually change the structure and function of our brains. This is because our brain is not a static organ - it has the ability to adapt and change in response to our experiences and behaviours. This process is known as neuroplasticity. When we renew our minds, we are essentially rewiring our brains to think and behave in new ways. For example, if we tend to think negatively, we can use techniques such as cognitive-behavioural therapy or mindfulness meditation to reframe our thoughts and develop a more positive mindset. As we do this, we are strengthening the neural connections that support positive thinking and weakening the connections that support negative thinking.

This topic of 'renewing minds' is a hot topic of discussion among researchers, and every year, hundreds of data are released in its favour. These medical studies have shown how a simple practice of intentionally changing our thoughts can transform our lives. This transformation is accompanied by changes in the physiology and chemistry of the brain. For instance, several pieces of research have shown that practicing mindfulness meditation can increase the thickness of the prefrontal cortex, which is part of the brain responsible for executive functions such as decision-making, attention, and impulse control. It can also decrease the activity of the amygdala, which is part of the brain that is responsible for processing fear and other negative emotions. This can lead to a greater sense of emotional regulation and a decreased risk of developing anxiety and depression.

In addition, studies have shown that engaging in regular physical exercise can increase the volume of the hippocampus, which is part of the brain responsible for learning and memory. This can lead to improved cognitive function and a decreased risk of developing age-related cognitive decline. Hence proved renewing our minds can change our brains by strengthening or weakening the neural connections that support our thoughts, emotions, and behaviours. By intentionally practicing new ways of thinking and behaving, we can create positive changes in our brains that can improve our mental health, cognitive function, and overall well-being.

So, you can see how powerful this method is of changing our mindset. The strength of transforming our thinking patterns can optimize our lives and level up our standard of living. We can beat diseases, enjoy successful careers, establish close relationships, get rid of addictions, be academically successful, win friends, and many other great things are now achievable just by changing the way we see, think and see the world.

Meet Sarah, a young woman in her early twenties who had been struggling with addiction to drugs and alcohol for several years. Sarah had tried many times to get sober, but she always relapsed. She felt hopeless and trapped in a cycle of addiction and self-destruction. Sarah's family encouraged her to seek help, and she decided to enroll in a rehabilitation program. Through the program, Sarah learned about the concept of renewing her mind. She was taught techniques such as cognitive-behavioural therapy and mindfulness meditation, which helped her to identify and challenge her negative thoughts and behaviours.

At first, Sarah struggled with these techniques. She was used to numbing her emotions with drugs and alcohol and facing them head-on was difficult. But as she continued to practice renewing her mind, she began to feel a sense of empowerment and control over her thoughts and behaviours. She learned to identify her triggers and developed coping mechanisms to deal with them in a healthy way.

Through this process, Sarah was able to achieve sobriety for the first time in several years. She felt more confident and in control of her life, and she developed a strong support system through her participation in recovery groups. She began to rebuild her relationships with her family and friends and discovered new passions and interests that gave her a sense of purpose and fulfillment.

In this way, renewing her mind helped Sarah to break free from the cycle of addiction and reclaim her life. It gave her the tools she needed to build a brighter future for herself and to overcome the challenges that had once seemed insurmountable. If Sarah could change her life, then you can too! No matter how difficult our struggles may be, we have the power to transform our lives by renewing our minds. It's not easy, and it takes time and effort, but with the right tools and support, we can break free from destructive patterns and build a better future for ourselves. The journey may be challenging, but it's worth it to experience the sense of empowerment and control that comes from taking charge of our thoughts and behaviours. And ultimately, we can find hope, purpose, and fulfillment by rediscovering the joys and passions that make life worth living.

Renewing our minds involves intentionally shifting our thought patterns, beliefs, and perspectives to create positive changes in our behaviour, emotions, and overall well-being. It's not always an easy process, but there are many techniques and practices that can help us to renew our minds and transform our lives. We have read several ways used by others to give their minds a new life.

Now, let's explore some more ways to conquer our mind and revive it. We will begin with Cognitive-Behavioral Therapy (CBT). It is a type of therapy that helps people to identify and challenge negative thoughts and behaviours. It's based on the idea that our thoughts, feelings, and actions are all interconnected and that by changing our thoughts, we can change our behaviour and emotions.

In CBT, we work with a therapist to identify unhelpful thought patterns and develop new ways of thinking that are more positive and productive. This can include techniques such as reframing negative thoughts, practicing positive self-talk, and using behavioural experiments to test out new beliefs and behaviours.

Another highly effective method is 'Mindfulness Meditation' and until now, and you have now become quite familiar with these terms. It is a practice that involves focusing your attention on the present moment and accepting your thoughts and feelings without judgment. It has been shown to reduce stress, anxiety, and depression and to improve overall well-being. To practice mindfulness meditation, you can start by finding a quiet place to sit or lie down and focus your attention on your breath. When your mind wanders, simply bring it back to your breath without judgment. You can also try guided meditations or apps that offer guided meditations to help you get started. And we just can't ignore the usefulness of gratitude journaling if we are serious about mind transformation.

Gratitude journaling is a practice that involves writing down things you are grateful for each day. It can help to shift your focus from negative to positive and to increase feelings of happiness and contentment. To start, simply take a few minutes each day to write down three things you are grateful for. They can be big or small and can include things like the people in your life, experiences you've had, or even things like a warm cup of coffee in the morning.

Now, here comes a more creative and engaging way (at least for me) to renew your mind. Its technique is 'Visualization,' which involves imagining a desired outcome or experience in vivid detail. It can help to increase motivation, reduce stress, and improve overall well-being. To practice visualization, simply close your eyes and imagine a situation in which you feel happy, confident, or successful. Try to make the visualization as vivid as possible, using all your senses to create a clear mental image. Besides visualization, physical exercise is also extremely beneficial for your mind. It is not only good for your body, but it can also help to improve your mood and mental well-being. Exercise releases endorphins, which are natural chemicals that help to reduce stress and boost mood. To get the benefits of exercise, you don't need to spend hours at the gym. Even a short walk or a few minutes of stretching can help to boost your mood and renew your mind.

Along with physical exercises, there are some other exercises too that will relax our minds and transform our thoughts. These exercises include breathing exercises or 'Mindful breathing .'They involve focusing our attention on our breath and slowing down our breathing rate. It can help to reduce stress, anxiety, and tension and to improve overall well-being. To practice mindful breathing, simply take a few deep breaths, focusing on the sensation of air moving in and out of your body. Then, try to slow down your breathing rate, taking slow, deep breaths and exhaling slowly.

Our discussion is incomplete without talking about 'Creative expression' and 'Affirmations .'It is a strategy that can help us to renew our minds by providing an outlet for emotions and thoughts that may be difficult to express in words. This can include activities like writing, drawing, painting, or playing music. Creative expression can also help to increase feelings of self-expression, self-confidence, and self-esteem.

While affirmations are positive statements that you can repeat to yourself to help shift your mindset and beliefs. They can help to increase self-esteem and confidence, reduce negative self-talk, and promote a more positive outlook on life. Affirmations work by rewiring the neural pathways in our brains, which can ultimately change our thoughts and behaviours. Some popular affirmations are "I am capable and worthy of success.", "I choose to focus on the positive and let go of negativity.", "I am worthy of love and respect.", "I trust in myself and my abilities.", "I am grateful for all the blessings in my life." To make affirmations more effective, it's important to choose statements that resonate with you personally. You can also try visualizing yourself living out your affirmation or writing it down and placing it in a visible location, such as on your bathroom mirror or computer screen.

Sometimes, our lives really get messed up and get out of our hands. We feel like nothing now could help us, and this concept of 'renewing our mind' seems like a fantasy or a myth. However, the reality is the opposite. Although it's not an easy task, and we may have to face several barriers to reach our destination but in the end, nothing is impossible, and we will definitely reach our destination. And remember, as renewing your mind can be a challenging process so it's important to have support along the way. This might mean joining a support group, seeking out a therapist or counsellor, or simply talking to friends and family members who understand what you're going through. By finding support, we can gain valuable insight and perspective and receive encouragement and motivation when we need it most. This can help us to stay focused on our goals and keep moving forward, even when things get tough.

Renewing our minds is a powerful way to take control of our thoughts and emotions and build a happier, healthier, and more fulfilling life. It is a practical concept that has the potential to transform our lives.

By proper support and using particular techniques, we can train our brains to focus on the positive, challenge negative thoughts and beliefs, and develop healthy coping mechanisms to deal with stress and adversity. Keep in mind one thing, renewing our minds is an ongoing process. It's not something that we can accomplish overnight or through a single technique, and it takes time and practice to see results. It's a daily practice that requires patience, persistence, and self-compassion. But with dedication, persistence, and a willingness to learn and grow, we can create a more positive and fulfilling life for ourselves and those around us.

CONCLUSION

Congratulations on completing the journey through "Master Your Mind" a journey to inner peace and fulfillment. Throughout this comprehensive booklet, we've explored the depths of the mind, uncovering insights, strategies, and practices to help you master your mental landscape and lead a life of greater clarity, resilience, and purpose.

As you reflected on the chapters you can acknowledge the progress you've made and the insights you've gained. Whether you've learned to quiet the noise of your mind, prevent burnout, or cultivate a God-centered mindset, each step forward has brought you closer to mastering your mental well-being.

Mental mastery is not a destination but a continuous journey of growth and self-discovery. It requires dedication, patience, and a willingness to confront the challenges that arise along the way. By embracing the principles and practices outlined in this booklet, you have taken a powerful step towards reclaiming control over your mind and shaping the life you desire.

As you navigated the ups and downs of life, remembering that mastering your mind is not about eliminating challenges but rather learning how to respond to them with grace and resilience. Whether you're faced with a noisy mind, burnout, or doubt, trust in the wisdom and tools you've acquired to guide you through the storm and into the calm waters of inner peace.

At the heart of mental mastery lies a deep sense of faith and trust in God. By cultivating a God-centered mindset, you align yourself with the divine wisdom and grace that is always available to support you on your journey. Surrender to divine guidance, trust in divine timing, and allow yourself to be guided by the loving presence of God in every moment.

As you close the pages of this booklet, know that the journey to mastering your mind is a lifelong process. Embrace it with curiosity, compassion, and an open heart, knowing that with each step forward, you are moving closer to the life of joy, fulfillment, and purpose you were meant to live.

May the insights and practices shared in this booklet serve as a guiding light on your journey to mastering your mind. May you find the strength to quiet the noise, prevent burnout, and cultivate a God-centered mindset that empowers you to live a life of deep meaning and significance.

Thank you for embarking on this journey with me. May you continue to grow, thrive, and shine your light brightly in the world. With heartfelt gratitude and best wishes on your path to mental mastery.